CUNNING
LATERAL
THINKING
PUZZLES

CUNNING
LATERAL
THINKING
PUZZLES

PAUL SLOANE & DES MACHALE

Illustrated by Steve Mack

**PUZZLE
WRIGHT
PRESS**

An imprint of Sterling
Publishing Co., Inc.
www.puzzlewright.com

Puzzlewright Press and the distinctive Puzzlewright Press logo
are registered trademarks of Sterling Publishing Co., Inc.

Library of Congress Cataloging-in-Publication Data Available

6 8 10 9 7 5

Published by Sterling Publishing Co., Inc.
387 Park Avenue South, New York, NY 10016
© 2006 by Paul Sloane and Des MacHale
Distributed in Canada by Sterling Publishing
C/o Canadian Manda Group, 165 Dufferin Street
Toronto, Ontario, Canada M6K 3H6
Distributed in the United Kingdom by GMC Distribution Services
Castle Place, 166 High Street, Lewes, East Sussex, England BN7 1XU
Distributed in Australia by Capricorn Link (Australia) Pty. Ltd.
P.O. Box 704, Windsor, NSW 2756, Australia

Illustrated by Steve Mack

Sterling ISBN 978-1-4027-3275-1

For information about custom editions, special sales, premium and
corporate purchases, please contact Sterling Special Sales
Department at 800-805-5489 or specialsales@sterlingpublishing.com.

ACKNOWLEDGMENTS

Thanks to
Anne MacHale for "What a Bunch of Cut-Ups,"
Davis Ryman for "Caught Red-Handed,"
Simon Downham for "Don't Tell Me,"
Ann Sloane for "Lame Excuse,"
Martin Schwenk for "Crossbow,"
Shannon Pennell for "Blood" and
"Two Wrongs Don't Make a Right,"
Ahmer Ali for "A Costly Trifle," and
Ian Charlesworth for "Eyeful."

CONTENTS

....

....

INTRODUCTION

There is a reason for everything that happens. Sometimes the reason is simple. Sometimes it is complicated. If we are to understand our world and the people in it then we need to understand the reasons why events occur. How do we do this? Well, many people make assumptions, jump to conclusions, or move quickly to previously understood situations and obvious explanations. They do not spend time looking for deeper or more complex answers. And so they miss the point.

It is said that when some Native Americans first saw a man on a horse they assumed that this was a new creature with two heads, four legs, and two arms. That might have seemed like a reasonable assumption to make, just as it once seemed reasonable to assume that the Earth was flat or that the Sun went around the Earth. The first explanation is often easy, obvious, reasonable, and wrong.

The purpose of these puzzles is to force you to look beyond the first simple answer. It is to make you ask questions, to use your imagination, to piece together clues and pointers, and come at the problem from different perspectives. This is lateral thinking. Your task is not to find just any plausible answer but to discover the answer given in the book—without looking it up! To solve the puzzles, have one person volunteer to read the solution and answer yes-or-no questions from one or more solvers. If you want extra help, a section of hints is provided. It will take lateral thinking, logic, creativity, and sheer determination to figure out what is going on.

PUZZLES

Secret Service

A spy wishes to transfer a large file of printed papers to a fellow spy. He does not wish to be seen in the company of the other spy, but he also doesn't want to risk the papers going astray, so he cannot risk mailing them. How does he manage the transfer?

Find clues on p. 50 and the answer on p. 72.

Clear-Headed

Why did twenty well-behaved middle-class boys suddenly shave their heads completely bald?

Find clues on p. 50 and the answer on p. 72.

Eyeful

There is a bee in my hand. What is in my eye?

Find clues on p. 50 and the answer on p. 72.

Stopper Shocker

A man died because a stopper was slightly too small to fit its bottle. Why?

Find clues on p. 50 and the answer on p. 72.

Nephews

Jill had three sisters. Each sister had three sons. Jill always sent each of her nephews a birthday card. Why did she send 11 cards to her nephews over the course of a year?

Find clues on p. 50 and the answer on p. 72.

Crossbow

Why did the fireman have a crossbow?

Find clues on p. 51 and the answer on p. 72.

A Chip Off the Old Block

Why did Jane always carry a potato with her when she went to work?

Find clues on p. 51 and the answer on p. 73.

What a Bunch of Cut-Ups

A man's friends all chip in to buy him a garment. However, within a few hours, he is glad when one of his friends damages the garment with a pair of scissors. Why?

Find clues on p. 51 and the answer on p. 73.

Easter Egg

It is a historical fact that in 1874 Good Friday fell on a Tuesday. How come?

Find clues on p. 51 and the answer on p. 73.

Souper Test

When Henry Ford interviewed a candidate for a senior position in his company he often took the candidate out for lunch and ordered soup for them. Why?

Find clues on p. 51 and the answer on p. 73.

This Sucks

A cleaner was vacuum-cleaning a room when she knocked over a small piece of wood. It was undamaged, but she was dismissed from her job. Why?

Find clues on p. 52 and the answer on p. 73.

Presidential Initial

Why did a U.S. president have an initial in his name that stood for nothing at all?

Find clues on p. 52 and the answer on p. 73.

Featureless

Everyone seems to think that they have them but nowhere in the Bible does it say that they do. What are they and what don't they necessarily have?

Find clues on p. 52 and the answer on p. 74.

The Driverless Car

On a dark and rainy night a hitchhiker was having no luck finding a ride. Finally a car stopped and he got in. But something was very odd—there was no driver! Suddenly the car started moving. The hitchhiker saw a curve coming up and reached for the steering wheel but a hand came through the window and turned the car. The ride continued, and each time a curve came, the hand reached in and turned the car just in time. Finally the car stopped and the hitchhiker ran into a bar, ordered a large Scotch, and told everyone what had just happened. Then two men came up to him. What did they say?

Find clues on p. 52 and the answer on p. 74.

The Deadly Brick

A man threw a brick through the window of a truck; the driver lost control of the vehicle and was killed. The police found a trace of DNA on the brick but there was no match on their database for the DNA sample. The man had no criminal record and his DNA was not on the police database, but they still caught him. How?

Find clues on p. 52 and the answer on p. 74.

Hot Date

Two people are handed the same undated newspaper item and asked to date it from the events it describes. One person cannot but the other person does so at once. Why?

Find clues on p. 53 and the answer on p. 74.

Hair Today

A man's three colleagues all have mustaches, but he does not. Who is he?

Find clues on p. 53 and the answer on p. 75.

Stand and Deliver

A man and his wife were sitting comfortably having a drink. Suddenly they both stood up and lifted their hands in the air. Why?

Find clues on p. 53 and the answer on p. 75.

Season Ticket

A man who is an avid football fan receives a season ticket for his favorite football team as a present. He does not use it for the first half of the season but he uses it for every game in the second half of the season. Why?

Find clues on p. 53 and the answer on p. 75.

Two Wrongs Don't Make a Right

A small theft prevented a large one. How?

Find clues on p. 54 and the answer on p. 75.

Blood

A man lies dead in a room. There is no visible mark on his body, but there are spots of his blood on the walls. How did he die?

Find clues on p. 54 and the answer on p. 75.

Handy

Originally it was based on the positions of the hands of a clock, but it has changed just a little since those days. It is still in common use today and is often seen on TV. What is it?

Find clues on p. 54 and the answer on p. 75.

Even Handier

A woman picked up a man's hand and held it over his face. Why?

Find clues on p. 54 and the answer on p. 76.

Caught Red-Handed

A factory worker is arrested and charged with a brutal murder after strong evidence points to him as the culprit. Later, he is implicated in several other crimes scattered across the country. He was innocent. What had happened?

Find clues on p. 54 and the answer on p. 76.

Don't Tell Me

If you suffer from it you do not want anyone to tell you what it is. What is it?

Find clues on p. 55 and the answer on p. 76.

Drunk in Charge

The police followed and stopped a car that was being driven erratically. The policemen asked the man to get out and then gave him a breath test. The man laughed—but he failed the test, as he was drunk. The policeman read him his rights but the man just kept laughing. The policeman said, "I am going to charge you with drunk driving." "You cannot do that," the man replied. And he was right. Why?

Find clues on p. 55 and the answer on p. 76.

Impossible

Because the sailors did it, we cannot. What is it?

Find clues on p. 55 and the answer on p. 76.

Profitable Business

A company makes a valuable product but uses that product to make more of the same product. However, it always makes a lot of money in the process. What does it manufacture?

Find clues on p. 55 and the answer on p. 76.

Social Climber

Starting at sea level, a woman reached the peak of a high mountain in less than two minutes using no climbing aids whatsoever. How?

Find clues on p. 56 and the answer on p. 77.

Reversal of Fortunes

A headline in the newspaper reads "UP GOES DOWN."
To what is it referring?

Find clues on p. 56 and the answer on p. 77.

Porpoise Purpose

In 1875 a porpoise helped Captain Matthew Webb become
the first person to swim the English Channel. How?

Find clues on p. 56 and the answer on p. 77.

Uplifting Experience

I went into a large ten-story hotel and took the elevator from the ground floor to the top floor. Nobody else got into or left the elevator until I got to the top floor, yet the elevator stopped at each floor. I did not press any buttons or request the elevator to stop. What was happening?

Find clues on p. 56 and the answer on p. 77.

Hopeless

Noales is an incompetent worker in a large financial consulting company. He is a complete blunderer who makes errors in all his reports, upsets customers, and comes up with hopeless ideas. Why is he retained as a well-paid and treasured employee?

Find clues on p. 56 and the answer on p. 78.

Spaced Out

The Americans spent several million dollars developing a certain space technology. The Russians achieved the same technology for virtually nothing. What was it?

Find clues on p. 57 and the answer on p. 78.

It Drives You Crazy

Why did a group of men request that the government provide them with chauffeur-driven cars?

Find clues on p. 57 and the answer on p. 78.

Refuse Refusal

A council proposed a landfill site for a certain area and environmentalists objected. Their objections were all met and gradually they all withdrew opposition except for one woman who refused to agree to the site. Why?

Find clues on p. 57 and the answer on p. 78.

Below Par

The world's most accurate and most poorly mannered golfer played the same course once in the morning and again that same afternoon. In the morning he scored 66, while in the afternoon he shot 77. The conditions were the same, so why did he do so much worse in the afternoon?

Find clues on p. 57 and the answer on p. 78.

Lame Excuse

A woman bought a pair of expensive shoes and then cut half a centimeter off one of the heels. Why?

Find clues on p. 57 and the answer on p. 78.

Polite

Ben was normally rude, abrupt, and in a hurry. He led a group into the park to have a picnic. They sat on logs and ate their lunch. He was then very polite and insisted on letting everyone else go first on the walk back to the car. Why was he suddenly so polite?

Find clues on p. 58 and the answer on p. 79.

Sorry—No Sale

A woman goes into a store to buy an expensive item. A short time later she leaves the store in a huff without buying anything, saying she has been insulted and will not return. However, an hour later she returns, buys the item, and departs. Why does she behave like this?

Find clues on p. 58 and the answer on p. 79.

Cube Root

Why did a woman put two cubes in a glass of water?

Find clues on p. 58 and the answer on p. 79.

Tap on the Shoulder

A passenger in a taxi tapped the driver on the shoulder to ask him something. The driver screamed, lost control of the cab, nearly hit a bus, drove over the curb, and stopped just inches from a large plate glass window. What was the driver's explanation?

Find clues on p. 58 and the answer on p. 80.

Speedy

How did Joe set a world speed record without being in a vehicle of any kind?

Find clues on p. 58 and the answer on p. 80.

Stampede

You are behind the steering wheel of a car. To the right of your car there is a sudden drop-off. In front of you there is a horse, behind you an elephant, and to the left of you a fire engine. They are all going at the same speed as you. How do you stop the car?

Find clues on p. 59 and the answer on p. 80.

Penny Pinching

A woman in a shoe shop tried on a pair of shoes. She then asked for the next larger size to try on. The assistant went to the stock room and deliberately chose the next smaller size to bring back. Why?

Find clues on p. 59 and the answer on p. 81.

Not Sick
••

A woman took her pet (which had a bad cough) to see the vet, but the vet told her that the pet was not sick. Why not?

Find clues on p. 59 and the answer on p. 81.

Pencil Case
••

A nightclub in Idaho provides all visitors with pencil and paper. Why?

Find clues on p. 59 and the answer on p. 81.

Interrupted Romance

A single man met a single woman and the two fell madly in love with each other. He took her phone number but did not contact her for two weeks, even though he was in the same city, had every evening free, and would have liked to see her. Why did he not call?

Find clues on p. 60 and the answer on p. 81.

Ram Jam

A goatherd noticed that his flock of animals was behaving very strangely. He investigated, and the explanation he discovered became the basis of one of the biggest industries on the planet. Why were the goats behaving so strangely?

Find clues on p. 60 and the answer on p. 81.

A Pointed Question

A woman took a blank sheet of paper and drew a single arrow on it. A few moments later she threw the paper away. What was she doing?

Find clues on p. 60 and the answer on p. 82.

Death Wish

A group of men was very hostile to another group of men and displayed this hostility in a threatening but nonviolent manner. However, before they could actually attack the other group, they all died as a result of their nonviolent display. What is going on?

Find clues on p. 60 and the answer on p. 82.

Rocket Science

How could a woman living in London drive her car to Paris in just half an hour?

Find clues on p. 61 and the answer on p. 82.

Undelicious

A man and his wife have dinner in an expensive restaurant. The food is first-class, the kitchen is spotless, the waitstaff is scrupulously clean, and the couple are not served any food to which they are allergic. Yet just after the meal both the man and his wife are violently ill. How come?

Find clues on p. 61 and the answer on p. 82.

Jack of Diamonds

A lab assistant who by night is a jewel thief has just returned to his lab with a huge diamond when he looks out of the window and sees several policemen entering the building. Trapped, he drops the diamond into a bottle on a shelf that contains an opaque liquid through which the diamond cannot be seen. How do the police get the goods on him?

Find clues on p. 61 and the answer on p. 83.

Carnage

The police did need not to look far to find who had vandalized a group of new cars but it took them a long time to figure out why he had done it. Why was it?

Find clues on p. 61 and the answer on p. 83.

The Deadly Deal

A woman looks in through a window and sees two men sitting at a table. Both of them are dead. One man has a gun in his hand and the other man has a pack of playing cards in his hand. What had happened?

Find clues on p. 62 and the answer on p. 83.

Unkidnapped

Why did a man report his daughter kidnapped when she was safe and sound?

Find clues on p. 62 and the answer on p. 83.

Blend to What End?

Why did a man mix chili powder with his paint?

Find clues on p. 62 and the answer on p. 83.

Birthday Treat

A little boy enjoyed his birthday so much that the night afterwards he had a dream that his family moved to a place where every day was his birthday. Is there a way his dream could come true?

Find clues on p. 62 and the answer on p. 84.

Lost and Found

A man was driving alone in his car listening to his favorite cassette when he accidentally ejected it from its slot onto the floor of the car, which was already littered with used audio tapes. Without taking his eyes off the road he rummaged under his seat, picked up the correct tape, and reinserted it. How did he manage that?

Find clues on p. 63 and the answer on p. 84.

The Bank Singer
....

A man in a bank begins to sing loudly. The cashier hands him a large amount of money. Why?

Find clues on p. 63 and the answer on p. 84.

String Along
....

Why did a man always carry a piece of string with him when he went out shopping or to the post office?

Find clues on p. 63 and the answer on p. 84.

Go Figure
....

Why did a man write the number 8549176320 on a piece of paper while his wife wrote the number 8549017632 on another piece of paper?

Find clues on p. 63 and the answer on p. 84.

Polling a Fast One

A man who hated politicians lobbied to have a "None of the above" box added to the ballot in an election. He was refused permission. What did he do instead?

Find clues on p. 63 and the answer on p. 84.

Short Trip

Why did a man take a plane journey from San Francisco to New Zealand and then immediately take the reverse journey from New Zealand back to San Francisco?

Find clues on p. 64 and the answer on p. 85.

Unlightable

A man wants to light a fire. The sun is shining brightly and there is not a cloud in the sky. He is focusing the rays of the sun with a magnifying glass on some dry paper on the dry ground. Yet he fails to light the fire. Why?

Find clues on p. 64 and the answer on p. 85.

Long Way Away

Maria received a visit from a man who had to travel a very long distance (and who wore a special suit for the occasion). Why did he make the trip?

Find clues on p. 64 and the answer on p. 85.

Moonlight Serenade

The police force has a strict rule that police officers should not take second jobs. The police chief saw one of his officers moonlighting as a security guard. Why did he not report him?

Find clues on p. 64 and the answer on p. 86.

Slow Progress

A snail is at the bottom of a well 20 feet deep. It can crawl up 3 feet in one day, but at night it slips back 2 feet. How long does it take the snail to crawl out of the well?

Find clues on p. 65 and the answer on p. 86.

Leg Pull

An eight-man tug-of-war team purchased an expensive new rope but had no other team to test it against for strength. How did they test it before they bought it?

Find clues on p. 65 and the answer on p. 86.

The Flaw

A graphic designer was very careful and proud of her work. She completed her design and then deliberately added a flaw. Why?

Find clues on p. 65 and the answer on p. 87.

QED

How did Archimedes, one of the first and greatest lateral thinkers, manage to sink a Roman fleet of ships in the Mediterranean?

Find clues on p. 65 and the answer on p. 87.

Pleasant Pheasant Present

A man goes on a pheasant shoot, but shoots no birds. Other people in the party shoot several birds. The man is a very good shot and has a loaded gun and permission to shoot. Why does he kill no birds?

Find clues on p. 65 and the answer on p. 87.

Money Laundering

A woman is asked to clean a house thoroughly for a very small amount of money. However, halfway through the job she becomes rich beyond her wildest dreams. How come?

Find clues on p. 66 and the answer on p. 87.

A Costly Trifle

A woman bought a newspaper to read. Why did it end up costing her over $20,000?

Find clues on p. 66 and the answer on p. 87.

How Odd

What is never odd or even?

Find clues on p. 66 and the answer on p. 87.

Eyes Wide Shut

Two golfers had a tie score on the 18th hole of a golf course, and were both on the green. Both missed their putts. The first golfer closed his eyes after he hit the putt while the second golfer never took his eyes off the ball until it stopped. The second golfer went on to win the hole. Why?

Find clues on p. 66 and the answer on p. 88.

Moldy Old Dough

Why did a baker deliberately add an ingredient to his bread that would make it go moldy in three days?

Find clues on p. 67 and the answer on p. 88.

Unusual Plumage

Why do some mother birds feed their baby birds feathers that have no nutritional value?

Find clues on p. 67 and the answer on p. 88.

Hire and Higher

A man was traveling in a foreign country and rented a car. Why was his bill at the end of his holiday much greater than he had estimated?

Find clues on p. 67 and the answer on p. 89.

On the Wrong Track

Why did a man persuade his friend to lie across the tracks in front of an oncoming streetcar?

Find clues on p. 67 and the answer on p. 89.

Refund Refund

A woman saw a shop with a sign in the window that read "MONEY BACK IF NOT SATISFIED." So she bought a coat but after a few days decided she did not like it. When she returned it to the shop the shop owner refused to refund her money. Why?

Find clues on p. 67 and the answer on p. 89.

Star Search

A few minutes ago, I made two five-pointed stars. Since then I have thrown them away. I do this nearly every day. What on earth am I talking about?

Find clues on p. 68 and the answer on p. 89.

Cool Calculations

A boy taking an important mathematics test was told that he could not bring any electronic calculator, computer, or book with him to the examination, but as a concession he was allowed anything else that would fit on a single standard letter-size sheet of paper. What did he do?

Find clues on p. 68 and the answer on p. 89.

Daylight Robbery

A man is stopped for speeding on the freeway. When he gets home, he finds his house has been burgled. Why?

Find clues on p. 68 and the answer on p. 90.

The Cab Mystery

A man takes a taxi from the airport and personally watches his luggage being stored in the trunk of the taxi. When he arrives in his hotel bedroom he finds that his valuable jewels are missing from his suitcase. What happened?

Find clues on p. 68 and the answer on p. 90.

Surgical Appliance

Why did a surgeon put a card with a big letter K on it on the top of the high cupboard in the operating theater?

Find clues on p. 68 and the answer on p. 90.

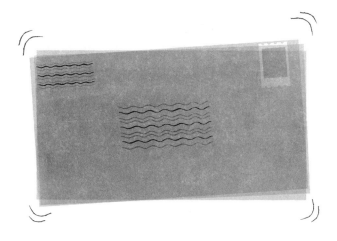

The Shaken Paper

A man takes a stack of paper, shakes it thoroughly several times, and then hands it to someone else who puts it in an envelope. Why?

Find clues on p. 69 and the answer on p. 90.

Dubliner

The golfing legend Ben Hogan was born in Dublin in 1912 but he steadfastly refused to play golf for Ireland. Why?

Find clues on p. 69 and the answer on p. 90.

Poor Value

A man sees an advertisement in the newspaper offering 100 cigarette lighters for $10. Why is he disappointed when his order arrives?

Find clues on p. 69 and the answer on p. 90.

WALLY Test

And now we present a test provided by the World Association of Learning, Laughter, and Youth (WALLY). Unlike the other puzzles in this book, which require thought and reflection, these are meant to be answered as quickly as possible. Give yourself two minutes to answer all nine, don't change any answers once you've written them down, then check the answer section to see how you did.

1. What should Donald Duck have been called?

2. What occurs twice in a lifetime, once in a year, twice in a week, but never in a day?

3. Why do Brazilian women own more shoes than Colombian women?

4. What would you call a young dog that had black spots on a white coat?

5. Name three types of car that start with P.

6. What does a woman do for a man before a date and a man do for a woman after a quarrel?

7. Who is the best-known unknown person?

8. What kind of fruit can conduct electricity?

9. If it takes one man three days to dig two holes, how long will it take him to dig half a hole?

Find the answers on p. 91.

Find the answers on p. 91.

CLUES

Secret Service

- He doesn't want to be seen handing something to the other spy.
- He packs the papers into a suitcase.
- He does not use a luggage locker because then he would have to get the key to the other spy somehow.
- He wants to use a location where picking up a suitcase is natural and would not arouse suspicion.

Clear-Headed

- They were all good friends.
- They did not do this in protest or as a prank.
- They did this for a good cause, but it was not for charity.
- They were not ill or suffering from an ailment.

Eyeful

- I am holding the bee.
- This has nothing to do with tears, stings, pain, or insects.
- What is in my eye is something abstract—a concept.
- The answer is lovely ... but it may make you groan.

Stopper Shocker

- He was an attempted murderer.
- He was poisoned.
- He had carefully planned his wife's murder.

Nephews

- Jill was not married and had never been married.
- She didn't accidentally send a duplicate card to any of her nephews.
- Each nephew got exactly one birthday card from Jill.

Crossbow

- The fireman took the crossbow to work.
- It might help him to fight certain fires.
- He would fire it at a particular target in a particular environment in a fire.

A Chip Off the Old Block

- She sometimes used the potato in her work.
- Her work did not involve food or art or agriculture.
- You could use a potato at home for this same purpose.

What a Bunch of Cut-Ups

- He was not particularly pleased with the garment.
- It was a jacket.
- He was due to get married shortly.

Easter Egg

- This has nothing to do with calendars.
- In the same year Good Friday also fell on a Thursday.
- Some people hoped that Good Friday wouldn't fall on that day, but were disappointed.

Souper Test

- It was an aptitude test.
- He observed what they did as they ate their soup.
- He wanted to hire people who would assess situations before taking actions.
- He didn't care about their table manners.

This Sucks

- The piece of wood was not valuable.
- The cleaner should probably have been told not to vacuum in the room.
- There was more than one piece of wood.

Presidential Initial

- The President was Harry S. Truman.
- He had no middle name other than S.
- This was not done for religious or political reasons.
- There was a family reason, but no one else in the family had just an S in their name.

Featureless

- They appear in both the Old and New Testaments.
- They are not prophets, apostles, saints, or martyrs.
- They are not human.
- They are seen in many paintings showing a feature for which there is no Biblical evidence.

The Driverless Car

- What happened was not a prank.
- The car was real.
- The car moved very slowly.

The Deadly Brick

- The man who threw the brick did not have a DNA sample in the police database, but he was traced through his DNA.
- The police did not get a full match on the DNA but they got a partial (or incomplete) match.

Hot Date
- The two people were of the same age and had the same skills and experiences.
- Neither had a greater knowledge of history or current events.
- The exact nature of the newspaper item is irrelevant.
- They were both given the same newspaper article but one person was given more information than the other.

Hair Today
- He is familiar to most people. You have almost certainly seen his image many times.
- He is not a real person.

Stand and Deliver
- It was not a hold-up. They were not in danger.
- They were not applauding or exercising.
- They were watching a sporting event.
- They were not trying to attract someone's attention.

Season Ticket.
- No one else used the ticket during the first half of the season.
- The team played all through the season and spectators watched them all through the season.
- The man would have used the ticket for the first half of the season if he had been able to do so.
- The man was in good health and lived at home throughout the whole season.

Two Wrongs Don't Make a Right

- The man who committed the small theft did not know the man who intended to carry out the large theft and did not know that he had thwarted the second man's plans.

- A man stole something of little value from his neighbor.

- A major burglary was prevented.

Blood

- The blood was his blood.

- No other people were present at the time of his death.

- He was not murdered, but those responsible for his death left the blood marks.

Handy

- It is not a timer of any sort.

- It is associated with one of the world's most popular pastimes.

- It is a method of recording.

Even Handier

- She was trying to help him.

- This is a routine test.

Caught Red-Handed

- His fingerprints were found at the murder scene—and at some other crime scenes.

- He was not a criminal.

- He was incriminated because of his work.

Don't Tell Me

- It is a rare medical condition.

- If someone tells you accurately what you suffer from then that induces an attack.

- It is a phobia.

Drunk in Charge

- The policemen were real. The car was driven on regular roads. The man was drunk.

- The man did not have special status, diplomatic immunity, or any other kind of immunity.

- The police followed the correct procedure for breath testing and charging the man, but he could not be convicted.

- There was something unusual about the car.

Impossible

- What the sailors did wasn't illegal, but it was irresponsible.

- It was fairly easy for the sailors to do, but for us it is physically impossible.

- What the sailors did happened years ago.

Profitable Business

- The product is in common use by everybody.

- You cannot buy it in shops, but it is not free.

- Very few companies are allowed to manufacture this product.

- It is a tangible, solid product.

Social Climber

- She reached the top of the mountain entirely under her own power.
- Mountains are found in many different places.
- She started from exactly sea level.

Reversal of Fortunes

- It is a financial report.
- UP and DOWN are not names or abbreviations of names for companies or people.
- A commodity is involved.

Porpoise Purpose

- The porpoise did not pull, guide, or lift Webb.
- He prepared carefully for his swim.
- It was a long swim through dangerously cold waters.

Uplifting Experience

- There was no attendant.
- No one else pressed any buttons.
- There was nothing unusual about the hotel or me.
- This only happens on certain days and in certain places.

Hopeless

- Noales is not related to anyone else at the firm.
- He could be fired for incompetence, but he is retained.
- They ask his advice.

Spaced Out
- It was a piece of communications equipment.
- It allowed astronauts to record information under zero gravity conditions.
- Both the Russians and the Americans already had something that would do the job.

It Drives You Crazy
- They all shared the same profession.
- They could all drive and they could afford their own cars.
- It has to do with the law.
- They were priests.

Refuse Refusal
- She did not object for personal reasons. Her home and family were not a factor.
- She objected on the grounds of safety even though no one but council staff would work at the site.
- She was the manager of a commercial enterprise.

Below Par
- He did not eat anything at lunch that affected his game.
- He played just as accurately in the afternoon.
- His poor manners resulted in his worse score.

Lame Excuse
- There was nothing physically abnormal about the woman.
- She was very famous.
- Altering the shoes helped her to do her job.

Polite

- Ben noticed something.
- Ben was thinking about himself, not others.

Sorry—No Sale

- She was not trying to haggle for a lower price.
- She wanted to buy with cash and the store was happy to accept her cash, but she stormed out and came back later.
- She was involved in a scam.

Cube Root

- The cubes are not ice cubes or sugar cubes.
- No drink or refreshment is involved.
- Dropping the cubes in the water could save her a lot of money.

Tap on the Shoulder

- The driver was reacting to the tap on the shoulder.
- After the passenger got in and gave his destination, nothing was said between them.
- The driver had only recently become a taxi driver.

Speedy

- His record was a physical speed record, but not for walking, running, or leaping.
- He traveled at speeds of over 600 mph.

Stampede

- Where would you find this particular set of conditions?

- If you are the driver of this car then you almost certainly do not have a license.

- It is an enjoyable experience.

Penny Pinching

- The assistant wanted to make the sale.

- The next larger size was not available.

Not Sick

- The vet listened to the pet's cough and agreed that it sounded bad.

- The pet was a bird.

Pencil Case

- The pencil and paper are given for a specific purpose, but generally speaking it is not expected that the pencil and paper will be used.

- The men who go to the club have all their physical faculties and can communicate. They are not expected to write anything down.

- The pencil and paper are not for a game, a quiz, data gathering, marketing, or promotion.

- The club had a problem obtaining a license.

Interrupted Romance

- He was not restrained in any way—he was free to come and go as he pleased.

- There was no other man or woman involved that would have prevented them meeting.

- For those two weeks he did not contact most of his friends, but there was nothing for him to be ashamed or embarrassed about.

Ram Jam

- The goats were more excited and lively than usual.

- Goats eat anything.

- Many of us now enjoy something as a result.

A Pointed Question

- The arrow was a sign but not for others.

- Once the paper with the arrow had served its purpose she threw it away.

- She was testing something—but not the paper or pen.

Death Wish

- The group who died was not murdered and they did not commit suicide.

- This took place in North America.

- The men who died were poisoned.

- The nonviolent display was a war dance.

Rocket Science

- We are talking about London, England and Paris, France.

- It was a normal car and she drove on normal roads.

- No time changes are involved. Her total driving time was 30 minutes.

Undelicious

- Some other people who ate at the same restaurant were also ill.

- There was nothing wrong with the food or drink in the restaurant.

- If they had had the same meal in the same restaurant on the previous night they would have been fine.

Jack of Diamonds

- The police are looking for any stolen jewels.

- The man refuses to answer any of the policemen's questions.

- The police search the lab and easily find the diamond.

- The police do not empty the bottles in the lab.

Carnage

- A line of bright, shiny new cars was bashed and vandalized.

- The vandal was found quickly because he had not tried to flee the police.

- The vandal damaged the cars out of anger and jealousy, but he did not know the owners of the cars.

- The vandal did not own a car or want to own a car.

The Deadly Deal
- They had been playing cards, but not as a game.
- One man had shot himself.
- They knew they were going to die.

Unkidnapped
- He knew his daughter was safe but he reported her kidnapped to the police.
- He did not do this to affect or influence his daughter or her mother.
- The police responded quickly and investigated the kidnapping. They were not pleased to find the girl had not been kidnapped.
- He told the police that his car had been taken with his baby daughter inside.

Blend to What End?
- He was going to paint one of his most valued possessions.
- He wanted to improve the protection that the paint offered.
- The area he painted would not normally be seen by anyone.

Birthday Treat
- His dream could theoretically come true.
- He would have to move far away.
- Earth spins around in one day and goes around the sun in one year.

Lost and Found

- All the tapes were the same size and shape.
- He had listened to most of the tracks on the tape.
- He could tell which one he needed by feeling it.

The Bank Singer

- This did not involve theft or crime.
- The cashier had never served this man before and did not recognize him.
- The man sang very well.

String Along

- He was an old man who did not have all his faculties.
- He did not use it for tying anything.
- He was cheap.
- It helped him to communicate.

Go Figure

- The numbers are not meaningful in the sense of being telephone numbers or account numbers.
- They were both asked the same question.
- They chose the order in which they wrote the numbers.
- They are of different nationalities.

Polling a Fast One

- He used other means to achieve his objective.
- He found another way to affect what is printed on a ballot.

Short Trip

- He did not particularly like flying and he did not visit or meet anyone else on the trip.

- He did not collect or deliver anything.

- The man had a phobia.

- He did this to avoid something.

Unlightable

- There is nothing unusual about the paper.

- There is no wind, rain, humidity, or other weather condition that would make it difficult to light a fire.

- He focuses the suns' rays accurately and they heat up the paper to a temperature at which it would normally ignite.

Long Way Away

- The visit was not a romantic one.

- His suit was not one you're likely to see someone wearing on the street.

- Other men have made the same long-distance trip, but very few.

Moonlight Serenade

- The security guard saw the police chief as well.

- The security guard knew the police chief wouldn't report him.

Slow Progress

- If it goes up 3 and slides back 2 then the snail regularly makes 1 foot of progress per day.

- There is a twist, however.

Leg Pull

- They did not use other people nor any vehicles or machines to test the rope.

- They wanted to put the same strain on the rope that two full opposing tug-of-war teams would produce.

- They pulled on the rope.

The Flaw

- It was an obvious flaw that anyone could detect.

- She did not introduce the flaw as a test.

- The flaw would eventually have to be removed.

QED

- He used science and simple weapons that cost very little.

- He did not use projectiles or boats or animals.

- This would not have worked on a rainy day.

Pleasant Pheasant Present

- No bets or financial motives were involved.

- The man was a guest.

- He was not a bird lover. He would have happily shot birds on another day.

- He did not want to show what a good shot he was, but this was not in order to make the other guests feel better.

Money Laundering

- She found something, but it was not money and it was not something that had been lost.

- The owner of the property was famous.

- She did not rob him or commit any criminal act.

- It was because she cleaned what she found that she became rich.

A Costly Trifle

- It was a regular newspaper.

- She made a serious mistake by buying the newspaper to read.

- It did not contain any misleading information and she did not buy anything, do anything, or take any direct action as a result of reading the newspaper.

- By reading the newspaper she caused a lot of trouble and expense.

How Odd

- This puzzle does not refer to something numerical or mathematical. It is literal and abstract.

- Read the question very carefully.

- Sometimes you have to look backward to solve a puzzle.

Eyes Wide Shut

- The two golfers were of similar ability, and both missed the hole with their first putt by the same amount.

- Both first putts went past the hole.

Moldy Old Dough

- He did not do this to sell more bread nor for any financial gain.
- He did this so that the bread would not last more than three days.
- This happened in Australia in the 19th century.

Unusual Plumage

- There is a benefit in their actions but it is not to do with nutrition.
- The feathers are eventually regurgitated.

Hire and Higher

- His bill was based on the mileage he had driven but the amount he was charged was more than he expected.
- It was a scam.
- The odometer on the vehicle recorded distances and it worked properly.

On the Wrong Track

- He meant no harm to his friend.
- They were involved in criminal activity.
- The tracks were outside a shop.

Refund Refund

- The coat was unworn and in perfect condition.
- The shop owner did keep strictly to the instructions on the sign.
- He always refused to give money back.

Star Search
- This puzzle involves food.
- The shapes occur in nature.

Cool Calculations
- The paper had nothing written on it.
- What he brought met the criteria set.
- If it had been allowed it would certainly have helped him pass the examination with distinction.
- It was not allowed.

Daylight Robbery
- If he had not been stopped by the police he would not have been burgled.
- The police examined his license, asked him questions, cautioned him, and let him go.

The Cab Mystery
- The taxi driver had arranged for the man's valuables to be stolen.
- The jewels had been taken out of the man's bag, but the man never saw anyone else touch the bag.

Surgical Appliance
- He wanted to test something.
- Any letter would have served—it did not have to be K.
- It would normally be possible for anyone in the operating theater to see this card. That is why he placed it.
- He was a heart surgeon. Most operations were successful but sometimes patients died or nearly died.

The Shaken Paper

- He does not like what the stack of papers contains, but he has not examined all of the pages.

- He is a publisher.

- He shakes the stack of paper to remove something that may be there.

Dubliner

- No political or religious issues are involved.

- Ben Hogan liked Ireland and had nothing against the country.

- He was not born in an embassy. He was born in an ordinary house in Dublin.

Poor Value

- He did receive 100 cigarette lighters.

- They were not what he had expected.

LATERAL SEQUENCES

What comes next in each sequence? Some lateral thinking may be required!

1. O, T, T, F, F, S, S, ?

2. J, F, M, A, M, J, ?

3. 3, 1, 2, 8, 3, 1, 3, ?

4. 3, 3, 5, 4, 4, 3, 5, 5, ?

5. 2, 4, 6, 30, 32, 34, 36, 40, 42, 44, 46, 50, 52, 54, 56, 60, 62, 64, 66, ?

6. F, 4, E, S, 9, S, E, 5, E, ?

7. E, N, A, O, L, S, L, U, A, ?

8. S, M, H, D, W, M, Q, ?

9. A, B, C, D, E, H, I, K, M, ?

10. 202, 122, 232, 425, 262, ?

11. C, D, I, L, M, V, ?

12. A, A, A, A, C, C, C, D, F, G, H, I, I, I, I, ?

13. B, E, J, Q, X, ?

14. F, S, T, F, F, S, S, ?

Find the answers on p. 92.

PUZZLE
ANSWERS

Secret Service

The spies travel by plane to another city on the same flight but sit far apart from each other. Each of them picks up the other's suitcase at baggage claim.

Clear-Headed

There were 21 boys in the class. One of them was diagnosed with cancer and had to have chemotherapy treatment, which made him lose all his hair. His classmates all had their heads shaved so that he would not feel out of place or unusual.

Eyeful

The answer is "beauty." Beauty is in the eye of the bee-holder!

Stopper Shocker

If you wish to poison someone, you can take a small dose of poison every day to build up immunity; this was the man's plan. He intended to kill his wife by putting poison in her food. To evade suspicion in her death, he would also eat the poisoned food; what would be a lethal dose for his wife would just make him ill. Unluckily for him, the stopper was loose on the bottle of poison. This caused the water in the bottle to evaporate over time, so the last dose he took was very concentrated and killed him.

Nephews

Jill had three sisters and one brother. Her brother had two sons, so she had 11 nephews in all.

Crossbow

In Germany there are specialized firefighters who work in chemical plants. To prevent barrels from bursting or exploding, they pierce them with the crossbow bolts to depressurize them.

72

A Chip off the Old Block

Jane was an electrician. She was often asked to replace broken light bulbs, but they are difficult to remove. She pushed the raw potato into the broken glass of the bulb, which was then easy to rotate and extract.

What a Bunch of Cut-Ups

The man is getting married and his friends buy him a straitjacket for his stag party. As a prank they leave him tied up in a locked room. He is delighted when his best man comes and cuts him free.

Easter Egg

In 1874 a horse called Good Friday was running in a race on a Tuesday. He fell.

Souper Test

Ford watched to see if the candidate put salt or pepper into their soup before tasting it. If so, Ford would not hire them. He did not want people who prejudged situations. He wanted people who would test first before taking action.

This Sucks

The piece of wood was a domino. It was part of an attempt to set a world record for the longest line of dominoes to be knocked over in sequence. The line consisted of over three million dominoes (they hadn't finished yet; the world-record-holding domino chain was over four million dominoes long). She knocked over one domino, which resulted in a chain reaction that ruined weeks of work.

Presidential Initial

The S in Harry S. Truman stood for nothing at all. He had grandparents named Shippe and Solomon who each believed he was named after them.

Featureless

Angels and wings.

The Driverless Car

The men said, "Are you the man who got into our car while we were pushing it?"

The Deadly Brick

The police got a partial match on the DNA for the man's brother, who had a police record. They checked him out and took his brother's DNA to prove the link.

Hot Date

One was a photocopy and the other was the original clipping. On the back of the original clipping there was a reference to an election that indicated the date.

Hair Today

He is the King of Hearts. The other three kings in the pack have mustaches but he does not.

Stand and Deliver

They were in a stadium watching a sporting event. The crowd started doing "the wave," and they felt obliged to join in.

Season Ticket

His wife gave it to him as a birthday present—but not being a football fan herself, she didn't realize half the season would be over by his birthday in early November.

Two Wrongs Don't Make a Right

When Bob goes on vacation, his neighbor Chuck steals his newspapers. Derek, the thief, is looking for empty houses to rob, but sees that Bob's newspapers are being collected and concludes that there is someone home.

Blood

The man went to Africa to study local wildlife. He lived in a small hut deep in the wilderness. He frequently got bitten by mosquitoes, which he crushed against the wall. Eventually, he realized that he had caught malaria from the mosquitoes, but he was too isolated to go for help.

Handy

It is the scoring system used in tennis. 15, 30, and 45 represented the quadrants of the clock. 45 has been abbreviated to 40, which is quicker to say.

Even Handier

The woman was a nurse and the man was lying apparently unconscious. Patients sometimes fake being unconscious. A good way to test this is to hold the patient's hand over their face and then let go. If the patient smacks himself he is unconscious; if not, he is faking.

Caught Red-Handed

The man worked in a factory that made Halloween items, including latex severed hands. He used his own hand as a model for the original latex mold. The product was just high-quality enough to retain the whorls of his fingerprints, and was used by several criminals to leave fake traces to throw off the police.

Don't Tell Me

It is the fear of long words, or hippopotomonstrosesquipedaliophobia.

Drunk in Charge

It was a British car, with the steering wheel on the right. The drunken man was the passenger; his girlfriend was driving.

Impossible

The sailors ate dodo. The dodo was a flightless bird first discovered by Portuguese sailors in Mauritius around 1507. It was hunted to extinction by about 1681.

Profitable Business

The company is the Mint, which burns old currency notes to provide energy for the manufacture of new ones. It always makes money in the process!

Social Climber

The mountain was below the sea. It rose from the seabed to just below the surface. She dived down from the surface of the sea touched the top of the mountain and then came back to the surface.

Reversal of Fortunes

The headline "UP GOES DOWN" is in the financial pages and refers to the fact that the cost of feathers has increased.

Porpoise Purpose

Webb was covered in porpoise grease as a protection against the cold.

Uplifting Experience

This was in Tel Aviv on the Sabbath. Orthodox Jews are forbidden to operate machinery on this day, so the elevator is programmed to stop at every floor to let people enter and leave.

Hopeless

They keep Noales well away from customers but involve him in internal meetings. They listen carefully to the terrible advice that Noales gives and then do the opposite.

Spaced Out

The Americans invented a special ballpoint pen that worked under zero gravity conditions in space. The Russians used pencils.

It Drives You Crazy

They were Catholic priests in Serbia where a new zero-tolerance policy had been introduced for drinking and driving. These men had to say mass in several different locations each Sunday and had to drive from one church to another after drinking communion wine.

Refuse Refusal

The final objector was the manager of a large local airport. Landfill sites attract large birds that can be sucked into jet engines and cause planes to crash.

Below Par

Because he is so consistent and accurate his shots land in the divot holes he left in the morning. This makes the next shot more difficult. Being poorly mannered, he had not replaced his divots.

Lame Excuse

The woman was Marilyn Monroe. In the train station scene in the movie *Some Like it Hot*, she wanted to walk in a very flamboyant way and waggle her hips. Having one heel slightly lower than the other helped her to achieve the effect. It worked so well that she cut one heel on other pairs of shoes.

Polite

Ben ripped the back of his trousers when he sat on the log. He let the others go first to avoid embarrassment.

Sorry—No Sale

The woman in the shop offered a $500 bill in payment for a dress. The shop said the note had to be checked for authenticity at the bank next door. The bank checked it and it was genuine. The woman said her integrity had been questioned and she was insulted. She stormed out of the shop, vowing never to return. However, she returned that afternoon and bought the dress saying she could not find it elsewhere. This time the $500 bill she presented was a forgery, but the shop decided not to have it checked because of their previous experience.

Cube Root

The cubes are a pair of dice to be used in a craps game. If they are loaded, they will always float to the bottom of the glass with their heaviest side down. This is a way of checking that the dice are fair.

Tap on the Shoulder

The driver explained to his worried passenger, "I'm sorry, it's really not your fault. Today is my first day driving a cab. I have been driving a hearse for the last 25 years!"

Speedy

On August 16, 1960, U.S. airman Joseph Kittinger ascended to 103,000 feet in a balloon. He jumped out, and on his descent he freefell at speeds up to 614 miles per hour, approaching the speed of sound without the protection of an aircraft or space vehicle and experiencing temperatures as low as –94 degrees Fahrenheit. He was in freefall for four and a half minutes before he opened his parachute at 18,000 feet. President Eisenhower presented Kittinger with an award for his feat.

Stampede

You cannot stop the car. You wait for the operator to stop the merry-go-round and then you get off.

Penny Pinching

The woman thought that the first pair of shoes was a little tight and asked for the next larger size to try on. When the assistant went to the stockroom she found that the next larger size wasn't in stock. She gave the customer the smaller size. Those pinched and the assistant then apologized and said "I'm sorry—here is the larger pair," giving back the original pair of shoes. These felt better now after the very tight pair and the customer bought them.

Not Sick

In this true story the woman bought a parrot from a pet shop. When she got it home it developed a bad cough. She took it to the vet who said there was nothing wrong with it. She then investigated its history and found that the parrot had previously been the pet in an old people's home and it had learned to copy the heavy coughs of some of the patients.

Pencil Case

The owners applied for a license for a strip club but were turned down, so they set up an "art club" instead. Customers were given a pencil and paper so that as they watched the dancers they could claim to be sketching naked models.

Interrupted Romance

He lost his mobile phone and that was the only place where he had her telephone number.

Ram Jam

The goats had been eating wild coffee beans that made them excited and jumpy. The goatherd decided to try boiling some of the beans in water and so the drinking of coffee was born.

A Pointed Question

A woman put a single arrow on a sheet of paper because she was testing out a new photocopy machine to see which way up she should put the paper to manually photocopy on both sides of the page.

Death Wish

One group of men was Native Americans who felt angry towards new settlers. They tried to intimidate the settlers by doing a war dance, for which they dressed up and painted themselves all over with a new and vivid war paint they had not used before. Unfortunately, this war paint contained cinnabar, a naturally occurring red, poisonous compound of mercury, which entered the pores of their skin, killing them.

Rocket Science

The woman was on holiday in France and staying just outside Paris so it was easy for her to drive into Paris.

Undelicious

The restaurant was on board a ship

Jack of Diamonds
The lab assistant drops the diamond into a bottle containing liquid mercury, through which a diamond cannot be seen. Unfortunately, the diamond, being less dense than mercury, floats on the surface and the police can see it floating there. (The diamond will not react with or dissolve in the mercury.)

Carnage
The cars had been parked on farmland. Because they were shiny and new their surfaces were reflective. A ram (a male goat) saw his reflection in the car doors and, thinking he had a rival, he butted the cars vigorously.

The Deadly Deal
The woman is a deep-sea diver looking through the porthole of a sunken ship. The men are sailors who were trapped and drowned. When they were sinking and realized they could not escape, they cut a pack of cards to see who would be allowed to use the gun they had with only one bullet; the other would have to suffer a slow death by drowning.

Unkidnapped
His car was stolen and he wanted the police to treat its recovery as a high priority so he said that his little daughter was in the car at the time. A major police operation was launched and his car was quickly recovered but he was subsequently charged with misleading the police.

Blend to What End?
He was painting the underside of his boat. Normally barnacles cling to the base of a boat, but the chili powder in the paint keeps them away.

Birthday Treat

He dreamed that he had moved to the planet Venus where the day is longer than the year. It takes longer for the planet to rotate on its axis than it does for the planet to go around the Sun. Every day would be his birthday.

Lost and Found

The correct tape was warmer because it had been playing in the machine.

The Bank Singer

This is a true story. The man was the great tenor Caruso. He attempted to cash a check in a New York bank but had no identification with him. A strong blast of an aria was enough to convince the teller who he was.

String Along

The man carried the piece of string with him everywhere. He was a little hard of hearing but too cheap to buy a hearing aid. He noticed that if he put a piece of string in his ear and the other end in his pocket, people spoke to him a lot louder!

Go Figure

The man and the woman are taking the same test. One of the questions asks test-takers to list the ten digits in alphabetical order as they are spelled in English. However, the man calls the smallest digit "zero" while his wife, who is British, calls it "nought."

Polling a Fast One

He changed his name to "None of the Above" and became a candidate.

Short Trip

The man has a phobia and hates Christmas. By taking a plane journey across the International Date Line at the appropriate time he can eliminate Christmas Day entirely from his year.

Unlightable

The man is an astronaut who is trying to light a fire on the moon, where there is no oxygen.

Long Way Away

The man was a lunar explorer. Each of the "seas" on the moon is called a mare (pronounced "MAH-ray")—the plural of which is maria (pronounced "MAH-ree-uh").

Moonlight Serenade

The police chief had been shoplifting when he and the security guard saw each other. The police chief returned the goods and walked out of the store without anyone saying a word.

Slow Progress

It takes the snail 18 days. It crawls one foot each day (after slipping back at night) but on the 18th day it reaches the top and does not slide back.

Leg Pull

The eight tied the rope to a very stout tree, pulled with all their might, and used Newton's Law that to every action there is an equal and opposite reaction.

The Flaw

She knew that her client always liked to prove how clever he was by changing something in any piece of work that was submitted. So she deliberately added an obvious error that he could point out, so he would then leave the rest of the work untouched.

QED

He used a system of mirrors and lenses on a high cliff to focus the rays of the sun on the wooden and canvas Roman ships, destroying the entire fleet.

Pleasant Pheasant Present

The man is a hired assassin. If he kills too many birds too easily, he may be suspected, so he deliberately kills none despite firing several shots.

Money Laundering

The woman has been hired by Aladdin to clean his house. She gives the magic lamp a good rub and when the genie appears she asks him for lots of money.

A Costly Trifle

The jury in a murder trial was ordered by the judge to avoid all media coverage of the trial. One of the jurors bought a newspaper. When the judge found out he fined her and ordered a retrial.

How Odd

The phrase "never odd or even" is a palindrome. It reads the same backwards as forwards.

Eyes Wide Shut

The second golfer watched how the ball rolled as it went past the hole. By doing this, he gained additional information about the line and the break of the next putt he had to make, and so his next putt went in. His opponent did not have all of this information, and missed.

Moldy Old Dough

This happened in Tasmania in a penal colony in the 19th century. Prisoners trying to escape into the huge wilderness that surrounded the prison would often hoard their daily bread ration to survive the journey. Making the bread go moldy quickly ensured that the bread would become inedible quickly enough that prisoners would not have enough food with which to escape.

Unusual Plumage

The feathers wrap themselves around grit, pebbles, bits of wire, and so forth in the baby birds' stomachs and are regurgitated, thus preventing the young birds from digesting harmful substances.

Hire and Higher

The crooked rental car operator fitted wheels that had a smaller circumference than usual on the car. These revolved more frequently than standard tires would have over the same distance, and this made the mileage seem greater on the odometer (which counts revolutions).

On the Wrong Track

When the actor W.C. Fields was unemployed and hungry, he and a friend sometimes stole food from grocery stores. These shops had a bell on the door that rang when someone entered the shop. Fields had his friend lie on the streetcar tracks outside; the conductor would ring his bell furiously to warn the friend of the approaching streetcar. The sound of the streetcar bell covered up the sound of the shop bell so Fields could slip in unnoticed and grab some groceries.

Refund Refund

The shop owner said that the notice referred to him and that he was satisfied!

Star Search

I cut an apple along its equator with the stem on top. This exposes the seedpod, the cross-section of which is a five pointed star. When I've finished eating the apple, I throw the two halves of the core away.

Cool Calculations

The boy brought his mother, who had a Ph.D. in mathematics, to class with him and had her stand on the sheet of paper. Unfortunately for him, she was not allowed to stay there.

Daylight Robbery

The men who stopped him on the motorway were not policemen—they were criminals dressed as policemen. They asked to see his driver's license, which showed his address. They passed on this information to their accomplices, who burgle the house (and can estimate how long it will be before the victim gets home).

The Cab Mystery

There was a small child hidden in the trunk of the taxi whose job it was to rifle through luggage and steal the valuables.

Surgical Appliance

The surgeon performed heart operations. Several patients who had recovered claimed that they had had an out of body experience during the operation and had floated high above the operating table looking down. He put the card on top of the cupboard so that the next time this happened he could test them and ask whether they had seen the card and what letter was on it.

The Shaken Paper

The man is an editor in a publishing company who is returning the manuscript of a truly awful novel to an author. He has read only a few pages before deciding it is terrible. However, he knows that authors sometimes include a hair in the manuscript to check if it has been read all the way through. He is shaking the manuscript to remove the hair.

Dubliner

Ben Hogan was born in Dublin, Texas.

Poor Value

The man received a box of 100 matches.

WALLY Test Answers

1. Donald Drake.

2. The letter E.

3. There are more Brazilian women.

4. A puppy. (You wouldn't call it a Dalmatian, though—Dalmatian puppies are born with no spots.)

5. Cars start with gasoline.

6. Make up.

7. John Doe.

8. Currants.

9. You can't dig half a hole.

WALLY Test is on p. 48.

Lateral Sequences Answers

1. E. The letters are the first letters of the numbers (one, two, three, and so on).
2. J. The letters are the first letters of the months of the year.
3. 0. The numbers represent the number of days in the months of the year (31 days in January, 28 days in February, and so on), one digit at a time.
4. 4. The numbers are the number of letters in the names of the numbers (one, two, three, and so on).
5. None of the numbers shown contains the letter E when spelled out. The next number not to contain the letter E is 2,000. (Any number that includes "hundred" or "one thousand" in its name contains an E.)
6. Replace each number by its Roman numeral equivalent and the sequence reads FIVE SIX SEVE, so the next letter is N.
7. P. The sequence is Paul Sloane spelled backwards.
8. Y. The letters are the initials of increasing lengths of time: second, minute, hour, day, week, month, quarter, and year.
9. O. The sequence is an alphabetical list of all the letters that have a vertical or horizontal axis of symmetry.
10. 728. The series is the numbers 20 through 28 with their digits grouped in threes.
11. X. The series is an alphabetical list of Roman numerals.
12. K. These are the initial letters of the U.S. states, listed alphabetically (Alabama, Alaska, Arizona, and so on). The next state is Kansas.
13. Z. These are the only letters which begin the names of no U.S. state.
14. E. The letters are the initials of the ordinal numbers (first, second, third, and so on).

Lateral Squences is on p. 70.

INDEX

About the Authors

Paul Sloane lives in Camberley, Surrey, England. He has been an avid collector and composer of lateral thinking puzzles for many years. He runs the Lateral Puzzles Forum on the Internet, where you can set and solve puzzles interactively: **www.lateralpuzzles.com**

Mr. Sloane has his own business helping organizations use lateral thinking to find creative solutions and improve innovation. The Web site is: **www.destination-innovation.com**

He is a renowned speaker and course leader. He is married with three daughters, and in his spare time he plays golf, chess, tennis, and keyboards in an aging rock band, the Fat Cats.

Des MacHale was born in County Mayo, Ireland. He lives in Cork with his wife, Anne, and their five children. He's an associate professor of mathematics at University College Cork. He has a passionate interest in puzzles of all sorts and has written over 60 books on various subjects—lateral thinking puzzles, jokes, a biography of the mathematician George Boole, insights on John Ford's film *The Quiet Man,* and a nine-volume *Wit* series of humorous quotations. He has published puzzles in the Brainteaser section of *The Sunday Times* of London.

Mr. MacHale's other interests include bird-watching (ah, so relaxing), classical music and Irish traditional music, book collecting, photography, old movies, tennis, quizzes, words, humor, broadcasting, and health education. In fact, he's interested in everything except wine, jazz, and Demi Moore. (Our apologies to Ms. Moore.)

Paul Sloane and Des MacHale are the authors of ten lateral-thinking puzzle books for Puzzlewright Press. More recent titles include *Classic Lateral Thinking Challenges, Challenging Lateral Thinking Puzzles, Colorful Lateral Thinking Puzzles, Great Lateral Thinking Puzzles, Improve Your Lateral Thinking, Intriguing Lateral Thinking Puzzles,* and *Brain-Busting Lateral Thinking Puzzles.*